TWO OR THREE GUITARS

Two or Three Guitars

SELECTED POEMS

John Terpstra

GASPEREAU PRESS □ PRINTERS & PUBLISHERS □ 2006

for Mary

Contents

The light is such that wire shines
arches upsidedown
                  post by post
loping along the shining road.

From the celebration of the Falls
a current of excitement lasts
till beyond the town ahead
                       where
it will stand houses round its maypole
make clothing in the Maytag dance
and keep the population up
                       past dark.

If we were at Niagara now
we could see where this business begins
There it is all rock
                water   rock
and the water's great
                     exaggerated fall
A change in elevation's one thing
but Lord, the volume of it
                     uncontained.

In June of 1859
Blondin on a tightrope
                   crossed the gorge
For eighteen minutes
he held the crowd
                suspended
in an air of hopeless disbelief
                   Water

turned white
Men fainted
Women wept
                    when, almost over
the hero performed a backward somersault
He stepped at last onto the dry ground
                    of their thunderous applause
Minutes later, fortified by celebration and
champagne and not just a little bit nuts
he scamped the way back like a squirrel
crossing the wire in seven
                         And that summer
did the same thing over
                         but blindfold
                    on bicycle
                & behind a barrow
They came from all over, to be contained
in the power of the place and because
of the man's
                    outrageous stunts.

Sometimes along this stretch
men climb the trunk
of a telephone pole
                    like it was every day
They go to play tricks
                    on the currency
to fix the stream
                    that rides the wire
that comes from somewhere
                    deep inside the gorge

that strides in strict formation
                         above the earth
                         beside the King's #6
              assuming the countryside.

Here on Millgrove Road, looking east
at 8 a.m.
              angles of the sun
electrify the air
                    the bright dominion
reveals shade
              delivers lines
of radiant particularity
                         across the yard
to house and barn
And from the porcelain hold
              a commotion of electrons
is orderly dispersed.

It's still morning. This chill stays on too long
for spring, feeling like fall, forcing me
inside. Outside the frontroom window the trees
suggest the suddenness of spring, and driving
through the northern half of Jersey these
three days, lost on branching roads, winding
in between the broken rolling ribs
the hills, I mean, and bumping into unmarked
lakes, something, at least, had taken place;
I know these roads, treacherous with snow,
almost impassable, two months back.

    (Their three day visit over
    they're headed north
                         like spring
            in season
                         every day
    travels twenty miles toward the pole.
    They'll overtake it long before
    they make the border
                         cross into Canada
    and wait in the city
    till the weather catches up.)

Watching the car swallowed silent
by a dip down in the road, standing
stunned by sudden disappearance,
the arm comes down, the hand slips
into a hip pocket, awkward,
out of use, and we turn to go
inside.

           Today might be best
back on site, measuring
an interval for studs, slapping up
plywood walls, nailing them fast,
keeping time with the sun as the day
flies past, the mind raging
with details.
                  A body
                        would warm up to it
regardless of the work that's being done
and soon enough this sweater
would be shed.
                  They,
                        in shirtsleeves,
are already halfway to the Glen.
Outside the car the trees are taking back
their buds, and all the world is stretching
wider in between and all the world is homelike
alien
         resistable as spring.

■ QUANTIFICATION

It's irreverent to quantify, but if
Christus told the truth
then all these blades are
numbered too
                earth hair

When Jim and I were on
the 7th
            Concession Road
Vivaldi's strings were making
summer from a tape deck &
we passed what must have been
ten acres of pure lawn
                    a dollar
a square yard
            the sign said
phut phut phut
the water arc'd, in half-
circles, back again
ten of them
                playing
the pressure
phut
     all the lawn
wet crystal twilight
backdrop of trees, it was
epiphanal, I said
evangel in black
            & green

    & no notes missing
   & all those strings!
                      he said
they play
         on horse's hair
the bows, he said
                are horse's
                hair.

I applaud these twins of five
because they are Dexter and Sinister, and without them
        I beat the air
because every day they perform their tasks, and haven't once
        thought to complain
because one day, while he wasn't looking, his partner met
        the blade of a table saw
because they work together, and if by chance
        one is forgetful, the other may suffer
because they are two of a kind, like thieves on the cross,
        belonging on either side
because I stand between them, as a mirror, and both of them
        must come with me
because I am not Christ, and shall not cut the one off
because I am an invalid, and cannot work
        the surgeon says, for five weeks at the least
because he knows his work
because he does what I was doing when it happened
        but as a hobby
because while stitching up he told me so, and carried on
        with needle and thread, all the while saying
        the man who has a wound like this
        deserves it
because the thread carried on behind the needle
because he continued to speak, and I was in a stupor
because when it was complete I took my hand home
        in a taxi
because nine other hands were in the taxi, and I
        nearly fainted
because he gave me drugs against the pain, which I
        neglected to swallow
because that night the arm which branched into that hand
        was propped up, perpendicular to the throb
because native drums beat against my fingertips

because in the wild forest of my dreams at last it severed
and was thrown to the sea
because it sailed through the air, and sank in the sea
because it did so slowly
because when I awoke it was resting on my chest
like a tree which is felled
because finally it had slept
because as I sit new cells are forming skin
around the wound
because beneath the senseless gauze all creation
yearns for this
because within a week the itch will start, to signify
life
because the doctor's stitch will be made redundant
because the fingers flex already a familiar expanse of wood
across the saw, and wait for it
because the ten of them delight in this
because the two are twins, at marriage in their work.

Beyond the bedroom wall, through the window
hurried birds are pecking freely from the feeder.
Sparrow, grackle, wren, and a stubborn squirrel
who won't scare will winter under the eaves.
We keep it filled to keep them trained to keep
you entertained, I guess.

                          What is it
this or that side of the pane
most captivates your eye? the yard out back?
great with late summer
                          Flora Dea
her last fling
                     or the perfect landscape pictured
here
          where to the left another photo
shows a brook and underneath is printed
The hart panteth.
                          Do you stop and drink
Cornelius, and then, revived, focus
for a time on TV? or do you count
tomatoes, next door?
                          They ripened last
month, hanging red moons in hundreds
keeping the missus busy, bent over
filling baskets, her fingers calm and fast
into the plant, her buttocks round and swaying
swaying round the garden ground.
                          Do you take
by the way
          any interest in women? Is it her
physique
          invited Nadia Comanech
                          up

onto the wall? She contemplates the mat.
Steady and precise, with a young body
she will wind between the branches of
the parallel bars, weave a routine from
pole to pole and land like a bird in
perfect perch

        scoring ten.

               Beside her
Mercury Morris concentrates on hanging
there, reaching out his fingertips
to meet mid-air a pass that comes from somewhere
off the poster.

          Remember that game? He jumped
for nothing, landed out of bounds, no yards
third down, they decided to kick, and one
of the sixty thousand gathered there

                 caught the thing
and Sunday evening brought a football home.

   One time at the stadium, hoping to watch
the Mets win once, the pitcher tossed a ball
from the bullpen that landed on your lap.
He signed it first, and there it sits, name-
forward on the shelf.

            Did he even play that game?
or was he, like you, consigned to sit out
all nine innings?

          Where does your contract stipulate
how much you may, or not, participate?

The board game stands propped

             perpetual
on the bed table. Seven letters
each, we drop words

                        without sentence.
They lie in our silence like cyphered conversation
like clues to character and chance, like trachs
through which you cannot talk, meals
through a straw, like staring out the window
round the room, like victory
                                like victory
for you
            I've yet to win a single match
against this monumental calculating patience.

    Say it, Neil.
                    What dire sentence left
the tongue of God the day you were conceived?
Bedridden
                born to the interrogative
you leave us stand, begging.
We scrabble for repose
                        while you
                wordlessly pursue.

Every day I go outside and is it
not nice weather we're having? I tell
the same joke. Every weather it's
the same nice I'm going on about

How dry
a drought is

It's only dust
                    keeps the dancing up
and only wind
                    keeps the dust up &

I ohmeohmyoh clap in time
our earthy dervish land bland sand

I want rain
water
torrents
floods

I want thunder and lightning & to see some clouds
so black they blot the blue blue blue so bad
you can't concentrate on the fact it's day

I want
a wisp
as big as my fist
to give me a hint of hope right out of the blue
but no
nothing

not a whisper of anything
between us and heaven.

□

         Disaster surely
shakes things up, starts you thinking saying
what would have shocked yourself yesterday
like today, praying, either it rains
                   Lord
     or Lord we die

    so who'll break first?

Forty Days & Forty Nights

It may as well have been for forty days
and nights that we were on the long Atlantic.
Two by two, with children most of us
we packed our bags, walked the gangway, waved
and leaning on a deckrail watched the sea rise
up behind us, top the dikes and take the lives
of loved ones, still waving, their raised arms
at last drowned in the flood of the horizon.
Choosing to go, we should, you'd think
be happy
         but added to that ocean
                          our own salt
and then, in quarters closer than the country
we'd just left, waited, walked the deck
for ten days ate mostly variations
on a theme of onions
               as layer by layer
our former lives were peeled away, until
there was only left the small sweet core
with which to land upon our Ararat
Quebec
       from where the train, a cattlecar
of Frisians, Groningers, and *luyden uit*
Zeeland
        took us all to destinations
pinned onto our shirts
               male and female
we had no names, just places we were sent
like mail from overseas.

And this may have been the land the third dove
found her branch of olive in, but it didn't
look it. We sing *I rest me in the thought*
of rocks and trees, but after fourteen days

I'd had my fill, filling the cursing farmer's
wagon with the stone and rock that dotted
all his cursed fields, and learned a lifetime's
worth of foul English, courtesy
that man, while piling up those rocks
as if they formed an altar to our God
as if I were about to offer thanks.
If I was thankful then, it was in silence
surrounded by the ever-growing trees
which stood beside the fields, their bare trunks
the bars of my selected prison
                                    my chosen land
this is not, I thought
                          my father's world
the *dorp* cozy, and in the middle of things
with family, friends, with her out visiting
instead of set behind the farmer's house
walled within a shed he'd used to park
his car, until we came (we have pictures
from this), with not a soul for her to talk to
in any tongue, on any day, except the children.

    And yet we walked one Sunday into town
and standing on the lawn of someone's house
took the photo we sent home, and without
saying *This is where we live*, told them
about indoor plumbing, how everyone had
a car.
            Was it the foolishness of pride, or
faith, that focussed the Kodak Brownie on
our family? We even smiled. Who knew
if it would be a snapshot of our future?
We felt the daily care, there was protection
from the worst; we ate, were sheltered, sometimes

had to laugh. Do I say it right?
                                    At times
we thought the humour providential
that I, scared to death of cows and horses
was sent to work a farm
                        that once, needing
lucht in de band of a bike, and wanting
to belong, I overcame my fear of *Canadees*
and boldly asked the man at the pump for sky
in my band
                        that two days later I drove
the coal truck from my second job, and dumped
a one-ton load down the basement chute
of the wrong house
                        and the next week
wasn't paid, but shovelled those lumps of black
back through the window, until I couldn't breathe.

That week it rained. For all I cared
it may as well have rained for forty days
and nights and put the whole place under.
I've never come so close to cursing, and what
prevented it I cannot say, but looking
out the cellar saw the same sign Noah saw
and knew at once it was that band in the sky
I'd wanted all along
                        to tell myself
                                        to tell
the kids, so some day they'd tell theirs
that He had saved, protected us for this
that we could show his glory, not displaced
in people who'd been moved from there to here
like shining stones of coal
                        starting from below.

(1)

Every week my father biked the twenty-
nine kilometres across the Afsluitdijk,
from Witmarsum south, to where
     the Wieringer Meer was
before they pulled the land out
      from under the sea
      revealing farms
to which he came, selling seed
the Zuider Zee his *fietspad*
the wind against his coming and going
the wind anti the cyclist.

Faced with gusts these headstrong Dutch
     bow head over handlebar
slow the genuflection
     spontaneous to the blow.
Gods will be gods, and in their element
     precipitate humility
but tension shows in these who resist
who dicker the wind's direction
who'd rather not walk
     pedlars of the practical
     the polder.

     God created the world
and one step down from sea-top
     they the Netherlands
impounded salt-water's bottom
     behind a continuous mound
crosscut the farmland
     sent fresh in ditches

tidied up (*netjes gedaan!*)
and sit in victory, round a table

                tea time from the fields.

    (2)

Evenings in town, the elders of economy
(my father one of them) attend

                consistory of the Inn
gather themselves in armchairs

                share cigars
and read the minutes of the day:
stiff-necked, spring-shy farmers

                hesitate to buy
before the showers
but sales will doubtless grow again

                like clouds
                off the North Sea
over the whole area

                from Zeeland, north
to where the men sit

                in Frisia-of-the-*toren*
                in Bolsward town
around the table of today's paper
and seed will fall from burlap bags

                like rain
                so much depends
                they say
on faith, a more or less

                reliable inclemency
in each mind lives

                the time to come
                the ones gone

though now, after that war
the guarantees they thought
                were God
are signed by government
                the latest laws
                require
that the future come in stages
the Zuider Zee be pensioned off
                in lots.

It was here, at night, he first heard
the other side of the Atlantic
                and thought to go
against her better judgment, for reasons
that were in the air
                not on the ground
                but did not think
once there, it would be
                cows he'd have to milk
                or fields
he'd have to clear of rock
from someone else's
                untended glacier
while mother meantime sighed
                drumlins and conifers
                without kin
somewhere remote, off highway number 5

   or 2, or 53, Aldershot, Brockville:
it was not until the last, that she
began to feel the least at home

(3)

and relaxed

        with *Chatelaine*, the *Ladies Home*
her guide into this twisted *taal*
her new tongue, the one
they all grew up on, here

        descriptive
of their ways, or better

        it seemed, their lack
this whole world feeling forced upon
the land itself, intent

        on something else
and everyone, at random

        flung to farms, to town
and only slung together, idly

        by all that wire
        dip rise dip rise
guiding the endless two-lane
that brought us to this place

        at last, though now, at
        least, she sits, at ease
the magazines, the lawnchair

        close within the orbit
of a wading pool

        an infant son in water
the earth her footstool
the rented sod, sloping

        toward the river
the one they all came in on

though not, of course, this far along
where it's only a mile across, and
he'd've had a time with this

           who leapt the ditches
           poled canals
he must think twice about this now
           mijn man, for this
is not so mannered-well
           a waterway
creation's not as engineered
           once you've jumped
and every available inch
           isn't gold
           as when
they'd all lined-up for days, the men, the boys
wanting parcel of that new perfection
asking land

           the fresh polder, its
           earth, as yet, unturned
the parceling-out
           done on paper
           behind a desk
the unrimmed spectacles which held the pen
looking up, reflecting the wide and clouded sky
reflecting, and not

           the face
           of someone's son
           who'd never live
           to farm
unless here.
        Here.

(4)

Iedere Zondag
                man en vrouw
walked along the path
                                s'middags, na kerk
wandelde langs de North Saskatchewan
van de Groat Road, west
tot waar het andere
                                big ravine
crennelled the river wall
toen het nog bos was
before the highway shot
                                too, through there, arm
                                in arm they walked
the perfectly undeveloped way of foot
through stands of second growth, or third
this garden of bush
                                maar net alsof
ze in de Prinsentuin liepen
                                lived still within
the Sunday stroll of several generations
the whole town arm in arm
                                not this
their present unincorporation
                                their town unmapped
population six, including the kids
the four of us, who were enjoying it
                                the water, woods
the one day he was home, and shooting
across their path like chipmunks
light on earth
                                unconsciously observant
                                of all emotive fact

heads poked down or up from perch on rock, log
forepaws holding stones
                              to skip the river, or
                              gathering stones
at places Dad would institute
                              where he'd stop, stoop
and begin again the dam, the one
we'd made last week, or
                              a different one, another
                              creek we wouldn't cross
but squat beside the clear, clean flow, and
more quickly than the water rose
                              change its history
                              each week again
toss stones across its path
                              one by one, or
                              hand-fulls of
each stone intent, upon
                              the piling up
and clatter of its own event:
                              the evening in Bolsward
her argument against, or for
                              the trip, the farm
and other work, more moves, more than once
the amber lights of rural homes grew more
and more remote, and then the day
he brought the Biscayne home
                              new car, and took us
                              even farther west
where every Sunday the family drove
                              to river park

and walked the afternoon

                  and water welled

behind a pebble dike
where we practised, played

                  claiming a little land.

When Rijk showed slides of Holland, Baroque
churches slid back and forth across the wall
lightly, as if their centuries of settled bulk
and all the gravestones surrounding them
like bees surround a hive
                                        carried no weight.
It *looks*, he said, *they're heavy to fly*—and fed
the bright projector yet another carousel.
We sat and noddingly inquired after
facts, while he went on about his love,
those glorious, for-the-most-part barns, where also
hayed the music, which he also loved.
The two are indivorceable, he said,
and warming in a language not his own
told us that his best, most deeply felt
and liveliest recordings were made within
their walls, that the fingerwork was play
and the solid, fugal air so simply ricocheted
the stone, the walls, that one mike caught it,
barehanded.
                    And no one doctors the result.
He turned the volume up and said, *This
you cannot see; this, I think escapes you here.*
And wondering where he'd get off, we listened
to his spiel on how the buildings and the pipes
were one, their marriage made in the *hemel*, by
none other, who lived there—in Holland, that is—
how death could not divide, and how the folk
who filled the pews had witnessed consummation, and
were still, he supposed, enraptured there, and added
a fuller spirit to the sound:
                                        or added,

we counter-posed, the farts and drone of bodies
who've sat too long.
                              But he meant it.
And though now the building's empty, and they
record the masterworks for organ as if division
exists, back in your room you'll hear the sound
of traffic through the window, the speaker, or
someone's snapping candy in the next row, or
banging the pipes, and as your mind begins to skip
on what's *not* been doctored-out, these days
of sweet obsession
                              the notes collect
on the balcony rail, abruptly lift, they soar
and you're pulled, weightless, up, there, and all
you hear is that air, those walls.

I say this now that he's gone, of course,
and he can keep his old world, which, in fact,
he did, has done. The love of one girl
drew him here, but didn't pan. He stayed,
thinking back and forth; was poor; when friends
bought a radio for his little room, it so much
embarrassed, he finally flew.
                              I think not more
again to life in Canada, he wrote.
                              And lives
not far from a town I might have been born in.

And from the loft of this unhistorical building I hear
that radio. It's playing so loud that his departure's
lost in distortion. A girl is walking, cradling
whatever-the-song in her arms, and with her neat

staccato stride she brings that evening and
his smug, cultivated rectitude beneath the window
and by, but in a hurry, pulling me along
until we're both receding up the road
into the larger sound, until we're one
with the indefinite pitch of traffic.

                              My love.

This longing to record.

Where the *plebs Christi* gather
when the *kleine luyden*, in a choir
                              psalmen sing
and one *vent*, four rows up, in the tenor line,
one tone-deaf Johan (come out this year again for it)
delivers to the pitch, note for note, a sound so far
from proper modulation, disruptive of our harmony,
that the colour of our praising changes ...

  Toch welbehagelijk voor Uw aangezicht
                              hopes the director, word
for word, until the tune ends, when he motions them
to sit again, and without a beat missed begins to play
a prelude.
            Now though he plays with great fidelity
to the written score and to the spirit of the composition,
as would make you think his heart and mind were united
and the concentration total, his thought meanwhile
is fixed on nigh
                boer Johan.
                          For this year, like last year,
he hoped to hear the song the score sung flawless in his
inner ear flawlessly *in koor gezongen*. But this year, and
last year, his invitation to join the choir extended
of necessity to the whole of the congregation.
                                  He could
count, he knew, on seeing a certain number of the same
faces, each September, when the season started, but
the filling out of four parts required a solicitation
not patient of discretion
                    WHO COMES IS IN
                              he wrote
for the bulletin. And it was through this open door
came the *weduwe* and the *timmerman*, the *onderwijzeres* and

her friend,
          the *zangvogel* with the crow,
Thursdays at eight, in the church basement, and with them
one Johan, who, by reason of strength, at 74, retired from
the field, and though he can say no
                    HALLELUJAH without that
the word should crack, severally, shows no such gap in body,
and looks,
          Mijnheer Van Koorster thinks and sighs,
     like to last Septembers without end.

The *dominee* intones a benedictive Amen
and then
          a closing hymn.

■ THE LOO

I read somewhere that this
part of the country was first
settled because of one,
that Father Louis Hennepin came
upon the building by accident
during his travels
along Lake Huron.
This was already in 1679
at a time when flush
toilets were considered too
indiscreet for most Europeans.

The cause of sanitation has come
a long way since those first
squatting moments in the bush.
It has been shown that we
are better drained than our parents,
are clean in areas of the body
hidden to science, refuse
lice on religious grounds.
It is to give historical
imperatives their due, that
a line forms for the loo.

We are moving more and more
indoors, and I am relieved
just to talk about it.

At less than two my daughter
is beyond all this, stands
on the beach, in the long
line of those

encouraged by the greatness
of the lake,
goes
where she is, naked
new to the world, and
thinking the way they used to
thinking empire.

■ A Ceremony To Dedicate a Tree and the Backyard It One Day Hopes To Dominate

This is to the sapling, on its second leg
and to its first few years, growing in a cultivated row
    of the same species at Connon's Nursery
and to every transplanted being, in a country full of them
this is to eighty years from now, when the tree will have earned
    the presumptions of ownership
and to more than twice eighty years back, when others
    were cultivating their presumptions, locally
this is to Mr. G.H.—esquire, no doubt—and the entire
    nineteenth century, who began the digging
this is to where he planted himself
to the section of land he bought and promptly divided into lots
and to his political connections, and those of his family
and to his unpopulated, not built, paper town
    which subsequently was declared the judicial seat
    for the newly organized district of Gore
this is to the money he saw growing on his tree
to Mr. George Hamilton, and his zeal for husbandry
this is to naming the location after himself
and to Catherine, Mary, John and the rest of his extended family
    branches all from the main, who vary in width
    from 22 to 44 feet, and are paved
this is to the first city in the nation born and raised
    on the speculation of real estate
and to the one-way streets of history, local or not
    and location injunctions against looking back

to this hole in the ground
this is to unveiling the root ball

this is to all the intervening years, wet and dry, the wide rings
    and the narrow, until we reach the crowning present

this is to how quickly and persistently the buildings and trees
    went up, came down, went up, come down
    as the years drove on to get here

and to this slender, tapered stem, with few branches
to niggling leaves, like skinny brick houses on narrow lots
this is to rectilinearity in all its forms
and to the original grid pattern of the original streets
    as they were laid out on paper and transcribed upon
    the landscape
this is to pathways in the bush, and the trees he went around
    to get here
to the first survey of this neighbourhood
and to the surveyor, with his one eye in the scope—
    he was half-blind or drunk
this is to the shifting longitude of his vision, and the eighteen
    inches too close to Greenwich that he laid each lot line
this is to the minute, or so, that he was off
and to us, who live a foot and a half beside ourselves
this is to likewise pinpointing an exact location in this slot-
    like yard to dig three feet down for the new history
    of adolescent roots
this is to eighty years from now, by degrees, minute by minute,
    in all directions
this is to the latitude of trees
and to this one

and to the sixty some-odd years back, when the street was planted
this is to William and Jean, and the forty-odd years they lived
    in this house together
and to Jean especially, who lived more than half again as many
    years here alone, after her husband died
to the witch, as she was called, childless, picking children's
    balls off the lawn, hoarding them

this is to the trees hauled down when the street was widened
and to the one warm day in March when the neighbour
 was hanging laundry
this is to the sad, peculiar sight of no trees along the street
to Mrs. Jean Preece, and the two handbags she carried
 one in each arm
and to the lilac bush, which listened as she spoke to it
this is for all the world to see, the neighbour said
 she was naked
this is to the starkness of the occasion

and to living in her place, in place of her
this is to a house which holds no secrets

and to the man who built it
this is to the man's empathy, his tacit understanding that square,
 level and plumb are inventions of the human mind
 not found in nature
this is to every oddball angle and curve, indoors and out
and to living geometry
this is to the branches we follow, and the landscape of
 individual lives
to the lay of the land
this is in appreciation that it still exists, however blown
 apart, straightened out, laid upon
this is to recent findings
to the three feet down I dug, too easily
this is to the steam trains of the previous era, which produced
 the cinder which was used as fill which I
 was digging up
and to the neighbour who said, "It's all fill," he said
 because a creek ran through the neighbourhood
 before the houses came
this is to a map preserved in the library, that

confirmed his story
and to its date, 1842
and to the present streets and alleys which run in
    parallel lines perpendicular to the original flow
    but record the same with a dip, a bow
this is to that running low point of the neighbourhood
this is to following where it goes, comes from
and to following-up this feeling, God forgive, that it
    isn't lost
this is to the source
and to earned presumptions
this is to Mr. Hamilton, his friends and backers, et al.
    they never would have guessed

this is to digging in
to eighty years from now

When I must come to you, o my God, I pray
it be in the early hours of that day,
and just as on these mornings I would rather sleep
I beg the lively company to keep
of kids, in Paradise, where rest and rising meet.
My eyes will open, I will yawn and stretch,
and to the children jumping on the bed
I shall say, "I am Johannes Terpstra,
and this is Paradise, at your pleasure."
And I shall say to them, "This house has many rooms,
its hallways are for running, take the stairs in twos,
and we'll play inside the mansions of our living God,
for all doors open to the treasures of his kinderlove."

Let me awaken with these children, Lord, in your home,
this offspring of your fondest word, who roam
the towered heart of day and lift it from the frame
our plans project; and let me be like them, the same.
I shall arise and follow the one who follows his nose,
followed by the sniffling sound of those who have a cold,
by the ones who dawdle and the ones who'd sooner shove,
by those who pile blocks in silence and those who love
to knock all such building down, by the bossy ones
and those who daily bear their brethren, by the talkers,
by the ones who, left alone, begin to eat the garden dirt
because they, o Lord, desire to taste of your creation,
which is good.
                Let it be with these kids that I awake,
perfectly restored, inside the house your design has made
for the halt, the lame, for those whose raw deformity
stands out: the unloved, or over adored.
                                And let it be
that angels guide our thousand feet upon the stair
to lead us into hidden access of the secret lair

of your delights: the preparations, boxes, reels,
the paper, crayons, the fountains of water, ferris wheels.
Pamper us there, for whom the faith is one, waking up
on this morning or that. O Lord God, fill the cup.

When I must come to you, I pray
it be at any time of any day,
and if my eyes were closed, I shall awake
now, to Paradise, having seen your grace
fall somewhat like rain upon this one child's face.

—*for a baptism*

Naked Trees

ADOLESCENCE

A sapling is no more than a tapered tube, a two-by-two. Six feet up from the ground it projects awkward-looking sticks left and right that end in bursts of leaf, bigger than expected. The leaves themselves seeming oversized, out of proportion to the skinny branch.

Incongruities. The forms of adolescence.

When it bends in the wind, it bends beyond the point you'd intuitively feel has no return. What business has wood being so pliant?

However, elastic as it is, and because it must, the sapling pretends to the tree it envisions. There is no turning back. Once it has raised its head above the undergrowth it mimics the eventual outcome, behaves as if the goal were already reached, as if its future were fully contained within it now: home for wildlife, shade of the nations below.

The absurdity of this is transparent of course, as obvious to the eye as the ultimate fragility of the stick figure itself.

Then, again, the wind blows.

A tree is the perfect foil to gravity; gravity and its insidious ability to make that sweet pull downward at the end of the day seem like desire.

Fruit falls from the branch, as do leaves, so we know at least that a tree too is subject to the law.

But with all its force and strength a tree goes unequivocally in two directions at once. Poised at ground level, it finds the air above free and unexplored and the earth liquid with possibility. The greater the pressure gravity exerts upon it, the stronger and more obstinate it grows. A tree refuses any single, overweening influence.

While living in complete compliance.

As one who is called both to the centre of the earth and to the sun.

Trees inhabit the world between geography and population, between earth and animal. A tree, on the one, hand, may provide that fixed point on a shifting landscape, a signpost, the welcome outcrop of brown and green without which your destination over the hill, across the fields (to grandma's house?) might not be found. But at the same time the flurry of leaves outside your window and that steady accumulation of rings flaunts a visible, increasing history: trees participate.

Trees are the stakes that hold down this dark tarp of soil and civilization.

Or, they are superfluous, ornamental, added on to the twin requirements of place, people.

It is the open otherworldliness of the individual tree upon the landscape that encourages us to see it as being, at once, so necessary, and so simply gratuitous.

The table around which we are seated tonight felt the chill of its own nakedness before we came together. And to be honest, so did we. These four legs elevate a surface that presents us now with an evening meal: fruit of the chef's afternoon. When our arms pass the bowls or reach for the tall cups of wine, or when they shift and move to the nuances of our conversation, it is possible to think of other limbs. And when our heads leaned back just now and everyone burst with laughter I wanted to say I saw a crown shaken by the breeze.

Perhaps it is the wine. But tell me tonight if we do not feel as large and heady as the gods.

These slim trunks, then, surround our feet. And the impression tonight is of being one together with our fellow creatures, up among their many shining leaves.

The location and number of stars in the sky is determined by the trajectory of individual branch tips, each of which bears responsibility for a single pinprick of light.

As well, the individual bent of each branch is the result of its having scanned the black dome for an unlit location.

These are, of course, preposterous hypotheses, and it is likely that only those who are willing to admit to an uncommon empathy with trees would ever entertain them.

In any case let it follow that when a tree falls the lights dim.

Indifference to what? A tree, for one thing, shows the greatest feeling for the wind, and is moved by breezes too slight to be felt on the skin. It could not be indifferent to the earth immediately at its feet or there would be no growth. It is not indifferent to the sun, which is filtered to the purest form of shade. And if it made light of the squirrels they would no longer travel its branches or inhabit its hollows. If a tree never minded the limbs severed from its body, their loss would not stand out so. And if it were inattentive to this urban environment its darkness over against the darkest blue of the sky tonight would not be so reassuring, nor the need for reassurance so strongly felt.

For a tree is the go-between, the arbiter, providing a continuity from heaven to earth to the waters under the earth. And is sensitive to any change in relation, however small: nothing passes by but is noted, dwelt upon.

Perhaps unhappily, a visible impartiality toward everyday events is the price exacted for this, for taking the intercessory role, for being attent to all, equally, and giving voice to all this swaying history.

For keeping time.

A tree asks nothing in return for what it gives: fruit, shade,
figure, timber....

A tree is brought to the lumberyard when its role has already
been clarified. Some are called to be wall studs, and others to
be joists; some to be decking, others posts. Two-by-four, two-
by-ten, one-by-six, four-by-four. Some are set aside and sawn
into planks for the wardrobe, the table. Some are called and
chosen to be sliced into sheets almost as thin as this paper, then
sandwiched together with other sheets and pressed flat. Four
feet by eight. Three-quarters-inch thick. Forty-two, ninety-five.
Delivered.

The need exists for further clarification. A truck backs up
the drive with the load. Meanwhile, standing in the doorway to
the shop, and using a scrap of wood from the pile beside the
tablesaw, someone pencils a small sketch, tossing imperial
measures about in his mind as a branch might its leaves.

It was a tree that first persuaded these hands to work the grain,
and silently stepped inside.

Also known as Manitoba maple, ash-leaf maple, box elder, or, less respectfully, garbage tree. Ubiquitous. Is not always allowed to consider itself truly a tree, as opposed to a weed, and is therefore unsure of its place. This lack of certainty is apparent already in its leaves, which have no single, distinct shape, but appear in several variations on a theme taken from both the ash and other, more decided maples.

In the more boreal regions of the country the Manitoba maple's hardiness has led to its being lofted to the level of an ornamental, and it may often be found lining city streets. Around here, however, they grow wherever there is no one tending the soil: in vacant lots, along railways, or between the fence and the alley.

Thousands of their little apostles twitter down to earth each year in a persistent attempt to convert the entire deciduous zone. Most are hoed down as young shoots in early spring by the gardeners, and this may be why the ones who do attain some form of maturity often have a surprised if not furtive look about them. Rather than grow directly up, they shoot off at various angles to the ground, as if they had taken a running start at treehood but could never have anticipated their present stature and feel ill-equipped to deal with it.

Full-grown, the Manitoba maple presents a case of the one that got away, or an act of charity.

> By Babel's streams we sat and wept,
> For memory still to Zion clung;
> The winds alone our harpstrings swept,
> That on the drooping willow hung.

This was our favourite Grade Eight song. We slowed it down to a crawl, drawing on every ounce of pain and sorrow that were in the words and tune, having found that our deepest thirteen-year-old feelings toward classroom captivity were being expressed. It was the hymn of choice each Monday morning when our teacher asked for a selection to start off the week.

> There our rude captors, flushed with pride,
> A song required to mock our wrongs;
> Our spoilers called for mirth and cried,
> "Come, sing us one of Zion's songs."

Then one Monday the teacher himself became overwhelmed by the potency of our feelings and refused to let us sing it again.

□

It is a bit pathetic, how naked the willow is to its one desire, how acquiescent to the call of water. If you were to take one of those branchlets that are drooping down, aspiring to be roots, snip it with the sheers, poke it into the soil somewhere and introduce it to the garden hose, you would likely have the beginnings of a tree. The willow simply can't help itself.

And so they gather at the river, or in the case I am thinking of, by the abandoned canal. Here they may give in completely, and in private, among their own. And walking among them you feel there is a definite seeking after solace that draws them into gathering together. Or perhaps they simply don't want to have to explain themselves all the time. Lying on your back, floating in a canoe along the edge of the canal where their leaves touch the surface of the water as gently and silently as a paddle, you feel that no explanation is necessary. And let the water take you where it will.

Let my right hand forget her skill,
If I forget to love thee well.

There is great beauty in the renowned sorrowing of the willow, an exotic beauty; the beauty of the exile. And its weeping is all too well understood by all too many.

Captain Kintail

(*A weekend get-together, in late June, at a lakeside camp. A summer camp,
in the traditional sense: large dining hall, with attached bunkrooms &
counsellor quarters; a few cabins close by, in the trees—each with a long
Indian name carved or painted above the doorway.*

*Though still standing, with its view of the lake, the old wooden dining
hall has been replaced by one made of concrete & steel, which has the look
& feel of an airplane hangar.*

*Enter the group that has reserved the camp for this weekend—their
seasonal retreat.*

It rains.)

◻

Captain Kintail lets the screen door slam,
"There's not one cabbage to be found in all of Kincardine."
That's Frank, of course, back with the groceries,
but missing a few heads.
                    "Somebody, *write that down*,"
says Suzanne, to which Ron, drawing deeply from his bank
of epigrams, replies, "Words falsify reality."
So where's his head?

                    Oh, look out! Fasten
your seatbelts, we're taking off. And let's step on it,
let's tear up the narrow road that threads
the lovely and serene mennonite countryside, and go
where Frank has called us. Frank the organizer,
the shepherd, who gathers all of the ninety-and-nine
who'll sign up, each year, at this time,
for the windward side of holy Lake Huron, to camp
just down the road from a town called Kintail,

a town too small for shopping, which is why he's back
from Kincardine, lacking the cabbages, though it's more
kith than kin in this cabbageless patch we hightail it to,
free of the city and our private lives, for a few
last days, this last long weekend of Spring,
when the endless pilgrimage of Winter is really over,
and the pursed lips of every branch have already opened
into the kisses of Summer. Yes, the leaves are out.
We greet the saints: the trees, the lake.
And slow down already. We made it.
We're here.

              There's lots of time.

But slow is right, for it will rain, rain,
day and night, drip and drizzle, downpour,
for in the press of last minute details
someone forgot to pack the weather.

                               He leadeth us,
he feedeth us,
             to him
we shall complain.
                 Frank!?

CAUTION: Horsedrawn vehicles use this road,
says Menno, holding up the signpost.

And the rain will be amplified on the roof
over the dining hall all that first evening,
its volume cranked up so it takes a while
to convince the kids and tuck them in
to someplace new. And someone will light a fire,
and as the tot socks and sneakers hang to smoke dry
someone else will say that this recalls
the Iroquois longhouses they saw rebuilt
at Crawford Lake, with poles and bark, and roots

for lashing, and that the homes were not this wide,
but higher, and domiciled several families, and all ages,
from pipsqueak to grandam, for twenty years,
before they folded, into
the earth.
                    "That must have been fun," pipes little Ann,
"can *we* stay here *all* the time?"

                              And later on
tables will be shoved across the floor, chairs set,
and the board games will unfold, the picture games,
word games, in which we envision and invent
our own definitions, these last few days, this last
long weekend of Spring, before the break
to Summer, and we'll play to the present
sounds of nature, that echo
off the roof, that fill this cavern
of concrete block, and ricochet the walls
up and down the narrower cavern hallways, leading
to the bunkrooms—
                    someone's left the door open.
They flood back in.
                    "Daddy, I have to pee."
The kids are so juiced for this weekend.
                              Come,
lie down, little lamb.
                    "But I'm afraid."
Be not. Remember, Noah floated. And if it
comes to that, so will we. We're safe.
Lie down. You're safe
inside.

    BALDERDASH! says Milton Bradley,
eavesdropping spokesman for the sopping world
at large. Just who decides which are the goats

that'll never make it with your sheep? Mercy!
please. We're in this, all together, lamb and kid,
float
      or sink—it's in the genes. Open up.
New word: think, *geep*.

               New words
confirm
      or falsify.

So where's *his* head?

             And the last car
of those who elected to come
pulls into the parking lot past midnight.
The cavern is quiet, the children all sleep,
but our gepherd knows his geep, that this lot's
revved-up by the drive, wants to frolic.
While others slumber he leads these three or four
through an open window in the clouds, down
to the water, and by the moon, where they will build
a second fire, of driftwood, flotsam
in the life of a lake, what
the lake retrieves
          holy
            and for a while
they will forget what's what, the clock,
that ticking observation of ourselves,
the blanket urgencies that cover us, would save,
that plot our habitation on the planet, our days,
and they will abandon all
             to dance
themselves and us
           upon that point
between the walls of wave and cedar.

And the water says
                              refresh
                    refresh.

And it will sound like the kids again,
their voices bouncing off the cavern walls
when they flood back in, four a.m.

                              Somebody,
write this down:
                    this shared accommodation
of distinct individuals, singles,
several families, all ages,
                              and the similar nights
we're wide awake, and hearing voices, listening
for our name, while the earth's other half
keeps watch,
                    these foreign snores
from someone-in-the-next-room's deep,
                                        snorkles
from the long lake they're crossing; the dreams
and nightmares of other's children,
their little factories of toes and fingers
making noise,
                    pipsqueaks,
like the very early morning sounds
from under the soffits
          in the trees,
                              how very vulnerable
each night
                    we volunteer to sleep.

And in the morning the children will run
through a drizzle they don't mind
to tell about the big fish on the beach

and the seagulls picking at it. That's
nature. *Gross.* And they will run
right to the edge of the water
where the waves are slurping at their feet,
attracted to it, while the seagulls wait
in the wind for something to happen.

But nothing like that will happen this weekend,
none will go missing, not one hauls off
down the drink, though they're off, unseen,
all day, through the bush, the field, the beach,
though Marty will say, "Maybe it's the seven years
we lived in Detroit, when it was called Murder City,
but I hate to let them out of my sight."

And there will be more talk this weekend, tales
of the near hit, of accidents, or the recent persistent
conniving pain, the lump under there, the sudden
slow death of parents,
                 and talk
of how impossible or not it is to dodge
these standard random shots
that are fired from who knows where
but seem so well attracted to human flesh, can come
through any window, plate glass, stained, or the old
wavy kind from grandam's house, and shatter
the held familiar view, and lodge in the body, or maybe
only the wall this once, but delivering a fright,
and driving those glittering slivers of hot
compressed sand into the skin,
where they just burrow deeper,
                        as if to find
an ever safe inside.

          Someone toddles in for a nap.

Is it that late already?
Lie down, little lamb.

                 And the rain will confirm
a kind of reality within this cavernous hall,
its echo amplify
                         our current preferred building methods,
choice of materials, our code requirements
for concrete block, steel truss, the zero-
slope roofline,
                  like a bunker's, hunched
low to the ground, sieged against
the earth, the sky, expecting
                              sirens:
it takes the tiniest fears and bops
them off the walls like pingpong balls
in a box.
            You must talk softly.
Don't think aloud.

                  Say what?
The lights go out.

Is everyone okay?
                  Is anyone
not hurt,
afraid?

            But the light returns, and the windows hold,
and it's still only the last long weekend of Spring,
and time is flying, as usual, it flitters and pops
like a moth against the bulb, and our lives are only,
after all, slowly dimming, like the days
to come:
            Summer's next week.

Mercy!
So where's his head?

And so we will finally break, I suppose,
I hope, and take off to escape the weather
within, seek cloud cover, direct precipitation,
feeling it on the face, unechoed,
and pouring through the roof,

                       cumulus. That's
nature,
        human's, trying to lighten up;
and headed down the path in rivulets,

                         water's
slurped beneath the bottom step. "That's
the old bunkhouse," says Wayne. "The last year
I camp-counselled here, they abandoned it
for the new one up the hill."

                      And so it swallows
continuous mouthfuls now
of streaming rain, grows sodden
round the foundation, is given to rot
and remembering

               the many summer coats of paint,
the soft shell of lap siding, and all
carved initials, deep affections
worked into the grain—

                 is taking them with, it goes
with this decline,
            and won't be shored against
a listing toward the cedar slope, folding itself
for a slide into the lake.
               It desires
to be driftwood, someday.

       holy

Something like that will happen.

                            Our bunker's up,
of course, on higher ground, is intended to always
go no place. That's instituted, six feet down.
This perfect ugliness is built to last
till we're all below grade.
                    Frank!?
                            Ding   Ding
Is it that time already?
                            And the geep will be called
from the fields, the beach, to gather out of the rain,
shove chairs and tables, and find their place within
the loudness, the hungry confusion, for lunch, under
the only shelter we've got—so lighten up, already—
and it's only once we're sitting
and the cups and plates are being passed
that we notice what's cooking, who's
to the right, who's left, who's dawdled
out of doors.
                    All seats reserved
for anyone, says someone.
                            And our gepherd stands,
off in the corner, arms folded, wearing his wild grin.
He's in his element. He's just so glad
this crowd's come out, that the weekend's not
a flop, he doesn't care
where we are, who's
we, or where their butts are finally parked;
                                    these little ones,
for whom, for now, it seems
the earth's at last enough,
                    their most common ground.

And nature's act will clean it up this weekend,
and the children will rush in to tell
about the big fish on the beach
that's gotten smaller, is only
head and tail,
                         its inner life
transfigured, ascended into heaven
with the birds of the air.

                         And washing the dishes,
Ann will flip consecutive clean plates my way, and say,
"It doesn't happen often, but when George
gets mad, he gets bigger. It's scary.
I feel sorry for those guys
he's up against, in Thunder Bay."
And given his physique, it's probably
to mythological proportions that he grows.
No offense. It suits the lake. His job is,
he maps Ojibway paths to higher ground, where
they don't build, but greet the clouds, the maker,
individually
                         envision time and place, call
the long names, become a people
seeing roots
                    draw
                              upon the long lie-down
of elders under the earth, the sky,
unsieged;

                         and would we could be them, be him,
by George, and outgrow all enclosure, the confines
of the Hearing Room, bulge windows
from their frame and talk a body
language those lifeless landgrabbing
bigwigs can maybe understand, larger

than one of the deals, their mines,
their dams,
                    and dance on a point
between the walls of wave and cedar.

                                        May I?
                    Music, please.

                    And later that evening
Peter will hear two guitars tuning together
by the fire. And he will whisper, "I hope
they don't play "Heart of Gold"." For it seems
wherever two or three guitars are gathered, there is
"Heart of Gold". His whisper, however, no sooner
said, but pongs across the room, translating
to request:
                    "I want to live, I want to give,
                        I've been a miner for a heart of gold."
Listen, Peter: recognize that drone? Not
Neil's singing, but where he took it from:
perpetual rain, or the low volume
of everyday, when even what
you do with pride or passion
wearies, and you hear that white noise
loneliness,
                    the background sound
that slowly overcomes all tune, grows
deafening, it won't let up, moves
nearer to home …
                        is where
the heart? you'll sometimes wonder,
                                        until you wake
one morning, crawl all fours to the cellar, map
a path to that northwest corner, where's
safe,

where's dry, and curl
in a very traditional pose.

Mother of God,
it can come to that,
this native being
alone inside.

live   give

And the story will come down to us this Summer
that a small town flooded, and a ten-year-old was taken
by the wild white water at the side of the road.
They saw her rushed through the open grate, into
the culvert, and screamed for her, small and lost
within cascading concrete. Someone wanted
to go in after, but it was hopeless.
They had to wait. It took
all afternoon and evening
for the raging to abate.
Her parents
couldn't rest, of course, but only think
our little girl, and remember
with a single-noted vividness
everything she'd ever said or done, what
she'd given them, what they'd returned
in love or fear or anger.
Come morning,
and she'd grown larger
than she ever was, or, perhaps
than they could ever let her,
and they found her,
then, that morning, alive, but cold,
and scratched, bruised, with stiff limbs
from how she'd clung to the barest crack

in the concrete, waiting, a crack
their adult fingers
couldn't grasp.

        "I heard my name," she whispered,
"inside the water. Mummy,

                I never was afraid."

And on the last morning of that last long weekend
of Spring, before takeoff, before we break
camp for Summer, someone will sit a baby
on the beach. The rain's let up, at long last,
so gather round, and we will dig a puddle
at his feet, pour portions of the lake therein,
and watch the pipsqueak dunk and play as the walls
go up and the moat fills and the twigs
begin to flutter from the turrets.
And this compulsion will not go unrecognized,
and a certain giddy behaviour will overcome
the inhabitants at this point on the planet
as we work and sing and the kid is enclosed
most beautifully.

        Hold it, folks.
A camera clicks.
        Somewhere in there is baby Chris.

And the water says
        retrieve
           refresh
and rounds the castle sand, its hand
the gentle one that also roams his hips.

And another story will come down to us this summer,
that twenty years ago, give or take,
it was just the two of them, living

on the moon, domiciled in a small room,
one window, on stilts:
a precarious existence.
                              They lasted out
their weekend, then left
that garden of dust, but when
they first arrived, remember
how everyone went out, looked up?
The earth was all eyes that evening,
                              and the sky,
and the two were far and away
too small and lost
for us to see, but they asked
if you recall, for a moment of silence,
and now Buzz says that as the quiet grew
enveloping he'd never felt
so strong the sense he was
                              a part,
which is when he ate the piece of bread,
and the wine, he said, sort of floated in the cup.

It's almost time. We leave at noon.
                              And right on cue
someone will open a plastic bag, and the kids will rush
to grab, and stuff some in their mouths, and break
the rest, tossing pieces in the air, over the water,
gathering seagulls as we pack to go,
as we dwell, already,
on the afterlife
of briefly living here,
                              envisioning
the long trips,

        inventing home,
this planet that we come from.

            "Look out, people,"
says Ruth, "Someone's been writing this down."

And where we ever were
our footprints are,
        like on the moon.

But this coming Summer could, of course,
totally eclipse our weekend and the moon.
Summer's like that, once the sun wins out.
And we can always question how and why,
whatever the weather, what precipitates, and if
the moon's a place
         whose influence is over
the lake, the waves
        of doubt and pleasure
we dance,
      and begin the pilgrimage again.

     Captain Kintail's taking names.
We know where's *his* head:
same time, same place, next Spring.

And counting down the kilometres from camp
a family pulls into the station. I'm at
the pump, tanking gas into a car
thirsty for the lake, and thinking how best
to rethread the mennonite countryside home,
when a fellow ambles up.

"How about
that rain?" he asks. His grandam stitched
and placed it on his chest: Barry,

this isn't self-serve?
                              "No, sir," he says,
                    "it ain't."

Words confirm reality.

Someone, I trust, is keeping a record of this.

The Church Not Made With Hands

For unto us
        in Aklavik
is born a child, in
          Attiwapiskat
   Gaspé
        Cornerbrook, Newfoundland.
And a son is given in
        Wetaskiwin
          Bella Coola
Flin Flon.
      And the future of the whole earth
is placed upon the shoulders of the daughter of
Tuktoyaktuk
      Tignish
        Swan Lake.
And the place of their birth is called
          Vermilion
Temiskaming
        Nain.
   Picture Butte

An angel of the lord appears in the night sky
over Rankin Inlet, over
        Iqaluit, saying
This shall be the sign: you will find the babe
wrapped in cast-off flannel, lying
on a bed of straw, in
        Esther, Alberta
in a winter feeding stall
an open boxcar, outside
        Kindersley, Saskatchewan.

And sure, several hours north
from Hogg's Hollow, just this side
                              Engelhart
you see a one, sleeping in its mother's arms
on the soft shoulder, where their car broke down.
And the dark highway shines
                              imperishable life
while helping them
                              beneath these northern lights
and driving on, through
                    Cochrane
                              Kapuskasing
                    Hearst
past Nipigon, and on
                    to the little town of Emo
Rainy River Region,
                    and least among the little dots
that lie scattered as stars
                    and litter the map
of Northwest Ontario,
where they're expecting you,
                    as in so many other
of these least likely dots
                    this expectation
also is, in
          Miniota
                    Pickle Lake
                              Ohswekan
     Glace Bay.

For unto us
For into all
        this night
is born a child, this night
                bearing each
and the places of their birth,
                  and nativity is given
                  every name.

I moved to Burlington in my sleep. I moved
upstairs, to Burlington, master bedroom,
down the long hallway from Hogtown. I moved,
and in my sleep it was a Sunday afternoon,
Open House. Strangers were drifting
room to room, nodding in twos
through doorways, and fondling the woodwork.
They moved across the wall to wall
as if all the earth were under their feet,
but I knew they would have to leave, I knew
that four o'clock would roll around
and they would amble back to the curb, turn,
and try to imagine bicycles on the lawn,
themselves coming and going up the drive.
They didn't know this was my dream.
And in my dream it was preordained
                              all this
was mine.

              I moved to Burlington in my sleep.
I don't even like Burlington. I don't like
the little picnic towns that clear their orchards,
their farms, make tableland of every undulation
then gorge themselves on housing.
I badmouth Burlington so strongly
my daughter now complains of headaches
when we're driving through.
                    But in my sleep
the big garage doors opened
and I was taken in, surprised
that they would have me, they knew
who craved this entry
into the large and tasteful kingdom
of his personal indoors, his furnished soul.

I moved to Burlington in my sleep.
It grew late. The rooms were empty,
the strangers gone; and I slept-
walked down the halls to the front door
and stood on the stoop of my dream
home, and saw

        many other people
having the same dream as me.
We were all asleep. We were
sleeping together, a quiet cul-de-sac
of landscaped infidelity.

        Tractor paths
still sank their ruts
into our rolled ripe lawns, and I know
in my heart the lousy truth, I know
there isn't room enough for everyone,
and the further we drift apart
the bigger our houses have to be,
and it's no excuse, I know! but I hoped
never to wake. Our grasses matched
so perfectly, it was
a rapture

        of green. I was
transported

        to Burlington ...

        What can I say?
Some are chosen, some
not. They're left
standing, stopped
at the curb, observed
through upstairs
windows, wide-eyed

        nowhere.

■ OUR LOVES QUIT THE PLACES WE BURY THEM, AND ASCEND

Yellow green, the willows are emerging first again
out from our colour-free past, whisper
how brown it's been, is yet.

                    Across the street
the magnolia bush, wild candelabrum, has set
pink white tapers at its fingertips, waiting
for the day to ignite.

               Everyone waits,
to see what will happen next, asks why
the leave-taker lingers.

               As the long dying weeks
of this latest winter slowly stripped us
we ate less and less, slept through the mornings.
Pinned to these weeks as we are, and knowing
the seasons, we accept this drawn-out ending;
but neither natural history, nor past attendance, nor
scriptured almanac prepare us for the always abrupt
brutality, the late storm screaming ice and snow,
or that quieter violence that intersects earth
at spearing lily head.

               All colour is contained in white.
Why shouldn't we prefer to pull that cover tighter
that the late storm drops and the third day
liquefies, revealing the ground, its sample resurrection
of crocuses, like brightened memories,

                             purple yellow wakings
from a death we should be glad of?

We live on the simple surface of things, have felt
the earth's floor not deflect, stamping our feet

to shed snow, no deep reverberation to trouble
our limbs, the core; till now—the ground cracks open
wider than a crocus head, and granted Spring
the earth has always had, our loves have quit
the places we had buried them. We see them walking,
and feel the earth that bears us reverberate
each step: the landscape's an event
more sea than not, that we
must learn to walk again
and trust
        what happens next.

                    Reach your hand.
This past half-season has taken us
like water, beyond reason and belief. We live
where water empties itself, rolls stone, or rises
as a hill; and the air breathes in.
                 Should it
surprise us you take leave to rise
again, intangible as vapour, caught up
as the cloud we're staring after, then witness
what we see: a hand, a rose, a fraying sleeve.
All colour is contained in shapes the wind will free,
that linger our delight and desolation—
                   and ours
are now your only eyes, this
your hand that's reached, let go, and these
your only feet, returning toward our lives.

I walked to the end of Dundurn Street,
to the quiet hind of a busy road,
where the bus loops. I walked
to the foot of the escarpment and looked
up, way, way up, at all those stairs.
And though they are wooden stairs
that make a nice wooden sound, and though
they lean endearingly to one side or the other
in a manner steel could never comprehend,
there are still two hundred and forty-six of them,
and before I was even halfway to the top
my legs had begun to feel lead-filled,
and the next step seemed a millennium away,
which, after all, it *was*, in a way, since here
I was, scaling the rocky old face
of mother earth, climbing her limestone chin,
her sandstone, siltstone, shale, dolomite skin,
terra mama, and all those labour-intensive layers
of her makeup, so that when I reached the top
I had to sit and catch my breath, and there
down below, was our little city, lying
spread out on its beach of glacial rubble,
sunning itself on a completely other
geological time, and I thought, well,
here I am, three hundred and fifty million years
from home.

        God! but it's been a while
since the foundation of the earth.
ALL THAT TIME!

          and no one to talk to.

    I was alone, sitting on the brow
of the Niagara Escarpment, and except
for the constant swell and surge of cars

coming up Beckett's Drive to Garth Street,
or going down, it might have been peaceful.
I tried to concentrate on Lake Iroquois,
or Algonquin, whichever prehistoric pond it was
that lapped and bashed against this wall, but
the sun had set, and stars were beginning
to tinkle in the sky like wind chimes,
and a million lights were coming to life,
car lights, street lights, porch lights,
bicycle lights, night lights, and people
in their dim homes were moving
room to room, switching lights,
so the whole lovely view
flickered, all the time,
like lively little tongues, like
the lively little tongues of lovers
in the flame of affection,
and I thought,
this is like Pentecost, kind of.

How is it we can barely talk to each other anymore?

Three hundred and fifty million years is nothing.
We're at least that far apart, sitting across
the same room. Switch the light. Is it
just me? Or where on this hardened planet
is there a hope our mutually exclusive, accrued
believings of the truth will break down, soften,
and flow together in the heat of some unimaginable
quaternary change? Or do we grow old this way,
waiting till the common weather finally erodes
these bloody unforgiving rocks
into a willing roundness?

There's nothing much
to say—and it gets so tiring, climbing
the endless staircase of our wooden
chit chat
            chit chit chat
chit ...
            If only the window would blow open once,
and the conversation catch, like fire, so that
we're both, we're all consumed, and the room
isn't big enough anymore, and we take
to the street, and talk and talk,
and the languages we've learned to cultivate
exhaust themselves, so we have to dig deeper
and break out other mother tongues,
and get a bit drunk, spilling words
we never said before, didn't know
we knew, and we couldn't tell how long
we'd gone till people stopped
on their way to work, wondering, "What the...?"
but then they'd join in too—because
it was contagious, it changed the face
of the earth, and these three hundred
and fifty million years
were like ...
            over.

        But here,
today,
        the words we use,
they fly, they arc
and dive through air, land

where we don't look, won't dare.
I pick up another, palm it, a stone
chip off the top of this cliff,
                              thinking
I should bring it back home.
Put it on the table between us.
Show you. Show me.
                    How hard it is.
How long it's taken to get here.

This was to have been about the old flames,
and what they've hurdled, how they've leapt,
and about the old, retired men who gather
at the indoor mall, and take their coats off
so they are free to spread their arms
and be expansive, expressive, like in Slovakia,
Estonia, or Hungary,
                              because that is where
they come from, and because all over the world
people are still speaking in tongues
they take to other lands, like this one.
And I may have gone so far as to say
they are a kind of evangel, these old, retired
Eastern European men, who added
to their number there that day, me.

This happens down past Barton Street,
by Kenilworth, that they stroll up
to one another across the tile floor
and slap shoulders, stand around.
Theirs is the easy, growing animation
that's geared to draw laughter out.
                                        Look,
it's all good news: they speak, it seems,
solely to get that rise from their compatriots,
that explosive laugh; which is loud enough, God
knows, and less polite, it drowns the muzak out.

And I might have said, at this point, "My Spirit
is poured upon all flesh,"
                              for these are the words
of the text I thought applied, prophesied, in part,
these men.

Flanking them, on either side,
are the rows of cubicle shops, with their young
sour attendants. Staff is sour because already
it is a slow day, and they are bored, and time
for them drips tick by tick upon their forehead
like the kind of torture you've only read about.
Add to which, they work for some megapolitan outfit
that considers them more than just a little lower
than the angels ...

              but our old apostles
pay no mind, caught up as they are in the dip
and rise of their own arcane, gregarious exchange.

What does this mean, that we hear a lively commerce
only they can comprehend?

                    They move on.
Their lollygagging group disbands
and wanders in a drifting, ragged line
out to where the mall opens up and the ceiling vaults
high over a tropic of doughnuts, tacos and pizza.
They reconnoitre a table,
                 and some of the men
sit, while others stand, one foot on the bench,
elbow on their knee, smoking, buying only coffee,
and gazing through the skylights, or into the leaves
of the large *ficus benjamina*, as if entranced
by the incongruities, this daily foreign action
they share with a tree, the conversations
steeped in godlike silences.
                A woman walks past,
her age the one they may have been

when the fighting began, around the time
they also may have met the one they married,
with whom they left home, who also survives
and stands not far from here, bent
over the sink, is up to her elbows
in the dishwater of old world manners,
consenting that these ancient breadwinners
dream dreams
                              if they still have the eye.

Husbands and wives, and a war
elsewhere, that is said to be over.
                                        I've heard
about their friends, the extended families,
whole towns that were undone, in ways
unspeakable, or too mundane, because
it was like that in Europe.

But there are no enemies here, and nothing
is foreign, and everything is.

The boys and girls who tend the shops
are almost all grown-up now. It happened
as we sat here. They've aged, at least,
perceptibly, in their dolled cages.
                                        And if this
were yet to be about the dancing flames
hurdling time and place, I'd wonder at
these sons and daughters, what their vision
says, for this is also in the text, and I would see
those stated, mighty works of God
explicable,
                    but also at the Centre Mall.

Our old friends will emigrate again, at noon,
to a hot meal. And through the fire and smoke
of the steel-making plants nearby, they'll carry
with them, jingling in trouser pockets,
only as many minutes as the world
is handing out today.

And so I never wrote it.
For the confusion of tongues and cultures,
commerce, peoples in their generation,
round tables rooted to tile floors, cigarettes,
styrofoam, and pot-bound tropical trees
reaching for the skylights

bested my glossolalia, simple as wine.

I'm God, she says, trying it on for size,
then giggles, can hardly believe herself.
What's so funny? we call from the hillsides,
our armchairs that hover over her play.
But like the grand old dame behind the curtain
who's overheard the menfolk gossip she's pregnant,
she turns her face to us, as if to say,
Who, me? Did I laugh?

From one horizon to the other
the landscape's a litter of drums and barrels;
the wagon's tipped over, everything's pulled
from the shelves, and Barbie, poor doll,
is naked again, and missing both legs.
It's a cruel world, even for plastic,
but we've seen this scene, that torso,
too often to be moved.

Listen child, if you're God, fix it.
Mend these bodies, straighten out our living room.
And we'll sing songs to you, we'll praise you
to our friends. I'd love to tell
total strangers the story,
how good you are, how well it is
you behave ...

                But shall I then, or ever,
love you more than me?
Come on, Sarah Kate, let's clean up.

And so I take my firstborn by the hand
and lead her up the mountain, step by step.

Where are we going? she asks, and I say,
We are going for a sleep—and this, for once,
agrees with her. But I never tell
the whole story, or say that every evening
she is laid upon the bed prepared for her,
or that her trust in me might be misplaced;
that I am bigger, but angels stay my hand;
or that instead of her or me the bushes
and the pens are stocked with animals,
because, it seems, our kind must make death.
And I haven't told her now is the heyday
of gods and their playthings, who chuck
all holy routine, refuse prayer, see only beasts
in her and me: gods of commerce, gods
of self, gods of God, for whom
the only sweetest smell is ours, burning
with zeal, or else another flame.
And I could name names, I could point, here,
there; I could say, "railway cars at midnight,"
los desaparacidos. I could tell her
every day
          we inhale
the ashes of the innocents;
their last, expired
breath—
          that it's in the air.

But the story's too much, even
for me, and I'm bigger.
I lead her only through the prayers
I dare to speak, and hope she sleeps.

Coming here today, still thinking of Anastasia,
who died, too slowly, half-paralyzed, poor rat,
dragging herself across the cage. A pet's
old age: interminably brief.
                        Built a box,
white pine, at last: long having wanted
to build one they might break out of, if life
rebreathed—or wait: it would return with them
to earth: same gift.
                  Wrapped it
down in the roots of the flowering plum.

Come, let us share our dead.
Animal. Personal.

                  Walking here, by Aberdeen,
Longwood Road, those raw old barkless columns of pine
occur. This one, then, stands for Anastasia,
thanks, who with the others, if you eyeball
down the street, is faithfully propping up
its sagging piece of sky. That's so the roof
won't fall in, again, though it feels like it has,
at first—it always feels like it has. But
they keep it up, the dead. They lean
this way and that, twist in and out
of our line of vision, but they're still employed,
these poles, these uncarved totems,
who stand for them.
                 And them's many.
The war goes, but undeclared, not well.
Taking the shortcut here the count's
already more than my recall: a few
aunts, uncles rarely met, the grandparents
on her side, and mine. Her father—

his heart attack, vacationing
in his homeland, overseas; and his sons,
her brothers, all three, who died too slowly
of their disease, which he by awful graciousness
had lived just long enough to see.
A person could learn to hate
these inborn muscular ironies, that push
and bully our simple intricate lives.
And she carries it yet, that part of her
that splintered when they broke away;
and one of the poles we go by
stands for her. The one, perhaps,
you saw me lean against, remembering this,
inventing, pretending
something to say.

                    They age in the elements,
these poles, these posts, these trunks of pine
stripped of all their clothing.
They line the way, stand by
to haul our messages, communicate
the latest or the last reports, to bear
our sometime recognition, grief and memory,
our invitation over the same earth we travel
coming to this place,
                    to give them name,
                    to share
our deaths,
who go,
      who also stay.

Autumn is heaven, unless of course it rains cold
and takes out the leaves too quickly, but even so,
there are days in Autumn you wouldn't barter
for a fortnight of Summer.
                              Summer can be hell,
with the furnace running full tilt, triple shift,
and the scenery's melting together, including you.
But each good day in Autumn is minted individually,
to be enjoyed unalloyed, and they increase in value
the closer you get to snow.
                              Poolside in August,
the sun catches every facet of your dive
and chlorine bleaches out all impurity,
so you can begin to believe what you've got
is deserved—
                              but Autumn is more persuasive,
handing out its mid-mornings, mid-afternoons and
early evenings unexpectedly, one at a time,
so you know not to think what's earned, but thanks.

Now, I know there are some for whom, understandably,
this is drivel: the shut-in, or -out,
those who recently found how ill they really are,
or old; those who didn't do it, but rot in cages
all the same, or those who did, with just cause:
all those, in short, upon whom gravity has the upper hand:
their days are one insupportable bulk.
                              And me,
tripping lightly from this line to the next—
I don't enjoy having to temper my enthusiasm,
but it does sharpen the edge.

Autumn has an edge too. There's always
that one last day, minted in November,
that is so keen and rich and new
you can't want for more, but
to spend it. Then Winter cashes in.

So, what a nice day! That wonderful late autumnal
slant of light, thin spun clouds, a warm
chill to the air. Right now you can hear
people crunching their way through the leaves.
They've taken their jackets off and tied the sleeves
around their waists, walking the trails
by Cootes Paradise, or in the valley,
just like the same people will again
in Spring, that other season in between,
when the great mother engine
starts cranking up again.

The engine shut down a few weeks ago,
and now we're coasting.

Every minute counts.

Devil's Punch Bowl

■ DEVIL'S PUNCH BOWL

How my arm encircled the small world
of your waist, as you stood
on the fence, on the edge overlooking
the Devil's Punch Bowl, its narrow
band of water dropping
into the gorged hollow, elbowing
around the boulders a good
two hundred feet below
our feet.

      How cold the wind feels
on all our open wounds.

            I haven't dreamt
of falling since I was young enough
to be your brother,
daughter.
      In that time
the falling always became
flying, landing softly—
                ef words.

I know what rocks awake
and men can do, now.

There is no true protection.

Forgive me.

> Seven stories, drifting in on the various currents
> of books, friends, newspapers and TV,
> landing one beside the other.

In the first instance we have a dour Presbyterian minister,
Who in the days prior to his douring
Enjoyed what his grown children cannot fathom.
He flew. Single-engine aircraft.
(Whether the ministry, or his family,
also preceded the douring, I do not know.)
What their future father most liked
Was the exhilaration of solo flight.
And what he most liked to do,
At five thousand feet, is kill the engine.
It was as if he had stepped off the edge of the world
And could breathe the atmosphere of pure solitude,
Gliding downward in long, silent S-turns,
The only sound the gentle wickwick of the propeller
Revolving in the airstream.

I like that: "the gentle wickwick of the propeller ..."
The Reverend's very words, lifted from the memoir he wrote
Upon retirement, where his children first learned the story.

In the second instance we have the Chilean habit
Of erecting two-foot high memorial grottos at the side
Of their roads. Adorned with candles and fresh flowers
These grottos of the Virgin Mary, like diminutive hitchhikers,
Stand singly along the highways and byways,
Or cluster at the more dangerous turns and intersections:
Wherever someone en route someplace else
Arrived at their journey's end.

The exhilaration of solo flight, and
The Chilean Virgin Marys-of-the-road.

In the third instance we have a first-person account
Of a nine-day retreat at a monastery, where the participants
Painted traditional, Eastern Orthodox
Icons.
        "This is not an art class," the director said,
"But an intense spiritual experience of deep prayer."
Our reporter, baffled by her words, incised, as instructed,
The first lines of the image onto the board,
And began to experience himself as also carved.
Deep, he writes, called to deep
Within him. Later, they painted a thin coat
Of red clay around the board's edge, and where
The halo was to be—halo, symbol of the spirit of life,
The director said; as *adam* is
The word for red clay.
                        But it was when they peeled
The gold leaf from its backing, and were required
To bend closely over their work, breathe deeply,
And allow their exhalation to form
Beads of moisture on the clay, to which
The hair-thin gold, symbol
Of the divine in ordinary life
Then would bond ...
                        It was at this point,
In the act of in- and exhalation over the red dust,
That our reporter lost his objective distance.

A propeller revolving, wickwick, in the airstream;
The candleflame of a roadside grotto flailing
        in the slipstream of a car; and
Breathing the warm breath of his own lost solitude.

In the fourth instance we have the knitted caps
Shawls and sweaters that create the bright wool aura
That surrounds the stone dolls, lined up in ascending rows,

All of whom look like fraternal twin offspring of the Buddha.
The doll-size figures fill certain Japanese temples
As well as the need of those who regularly travel the path
To visit the miscarried, stillborn or
Aborted ones whose names they have inscribed upon
Their adopted stone.

At five thousand feet, breathing deeply,
    having stepped off the edge of the earth;
The Queen of Heaven presiding over the anonymous place
    where, by their own or another's liability,
    or by accident, someone was lost;
The windborne, thin leaf of divinity
    clinging to the red mud along the path; and
Innumerable Buddhas.

In the fifth instance we have one Wednesday evening,
At choir rehearsal, when the realization struck
That my fellow tenor, whose company,
Over and above simple acquaintance,
I had come so to enjoy, in ways that called deeply—
When his age (he was about to enjoy a birthday)
Was entered beside our years of marriage,
Could have been him—
He could have been our son.

One, not-yet Presbyterian minister, unattached, exhilarating
    in the limitless present;
Two Chilean mothers, kneeling
    in an intense experience of deep solitude;
Three dew drops of human breath;
The temple choir of the child Buddha; and
A solo tenor, exhaling
    the organized noise of the spirit.

In the sixth instance we have the Scottish saint, Cuthbert,
Who did not want to leave his island, ever;
Who, when he passed over, left behind the island
His body became.
                    Those stranded by his departure
Bought the best cotton money could find,
Whose purchase served also to confirm,
Coincidentally (as commerce sometimes can),
That nothing—nor death, nor life—
Can separate us:
                they found themselves
Clothing the absence of this saint of the western isles
In a shroud whose corner its maker had signed,
Weaving through the fabric
In cantering swords of Arabic,
    There is one God, and His name is Allah.

So. We have
One young saint, child to the Reverend father, restarting
    the engine, quitting his island of air;
We have the hurled, the tumbled, the crashlanded and torn,
    where they left their bodies;
We have the act, or art, of divinity,
    as applied to red clay, cotton;
We have pet names written in stone
    from before and after the moment, or not, of birth;
We have tenor and bass, alto and soprano, four parts
    like four horses cantering in the airstream; and
We have the sheer physical persistence of Cuthbert,
    who left and did not leave the limitless present.

In the seventh and final instance we have a second aircraft,
A glider, a model built of a scale of one-to-ten,
The product of one man's hundreds-of-hours

And a working tolerance of one-one-thousandths of an inch.
Nothing I have ever done or made comes close to
His attention to detail. Ah! and what of all
The other many things, for which
Is it ever possible to atone?
The glider is ground controlled at takeoff, and upwards,
Until it reaches a predetermined altitude, at which time
The engine cuts out and the craft glides a silent
Gentle parade of circles,
Returning to its maker.
                        Or not. Now,
Whether it came from human or some other error,
Or was due to some quirk in the airstream, I do not know,
But on its maiden flight this particular craft
Required that its maker watch, powerless,
In an intense spiritual experience of ascending spirals,
As his perfect handiwork rose, and rose,
To be the tiny speck
That one blink finally granted
Blue heaven.

Hearing this story for the first time I was both
        appalled and exhilarated.
Now inside its cargo hold
        I would wish to place each one.

■ To God, as a Small Pest

The squirrel scrambling, light-as-air, over the roof
is you, is it not? The roaming slope
to peak, across and down, scritches
delicate as destruction,
                                        shows that old animal
spirit trying to find a way in, never yet
poking a grey head past the edge of the skylight,
so I may see.

                    I believe, now,
you have no pride; an imagination
that ranges wildly, seizing any
shape that fits, adopting
what'll do,
                    with a relentless playfulness,
and your insidious intent;
                                        and I resist
this recognition, as strongly
as the gnawing at my fascia, soffit,
that I imagine comes next, and tense and listen for.

        I rather looked for you in the birds gathered
about the feeder, the many separate
thoughts one has, the argue and agreement
of wings, and a hungry abandon to the truth
of contending against another winter's advent.

New this Fall is the balled nest of leaves no bird
comes near, that the highest-reaching branches of the ash
lift eye level to the attic room I hole in.
You're home. Comfort and warning
co-habit,

as when I stood below, preparing
breakfast, and happened to look, you
halfway up the trunk, our eyes locked
and I wondered what,

what was that small round
black thing
you held in your mouth?

to my parents,
on their fiftieth anniversary,
and to their generation—
the war that ended,
and a weekly paper that began
serving their immigrant community,
also fifty years ago.

The night the lights went out we drew the curtains back
to let the sun, reflecting off the moon, reflect against
the snow as well, and into the room.
                                    Flooded
in that whiteness, our candle seemed to specify
the time and place, as the wick's tenuous grip
on the flame made puppet-dancing shadows
of our plight.
                Two generations in the dark;
a third asleep, upstairs.

And you told us a story we'd never heard, Mom,
about the visit to your boyfriend's home
to see his folks, who'd soon be yours as well,
in the heart of the countryside, in the heart of a war,
when there also was no light; no light was allowed
to pinpoint where you sat below the bombers
flying west across the channel, or the ones droning inland,
eastward to German towns.
                            Odd, these in-betweens
and opposites. It was your home which could betray you;
but there, within its learned familiar safety,
where curtains enclosed against the night,
you drew the curtains back, exposing yourselves,
to let the outside darkness marry
the one that filled the room,
and not be given, nor give yourselves away.

It was New Year's Eve, the end of the year
before the war's end. The sun's reflection off the moon
reflected a thin manna of snow, and too, you told us,
a flock of sheep—sheep!—that herded past
the house, along the road, but briefly,
wonderful and bold, reflecting
to your scriptured eyes
                                        what little light
they could not help but do.

The story almost slipped past me at first,
before I called it back. Now it seems
that all the lines of type that have been set,
and all the letters that were sent, the books
and phone calls, photographs, anniversaries and recent
hospital visits,
                                in all the fifty years since then,
have gathered in that room: the small Witmarsum
living room, and ours, here, around a story
you might never have said, had not the power failed.

Fathers and mothers are one
strange creature, who with their children can be
inscrutable, as some say God is.
Mother in kitchen fixes a silent dinner, her back
to the world, not speaking; angered or betrayed
by some unknown he's said, perhaps,
or we've done.
                        Father, prototype, sits in his chair,
reading the news on sheets of print
that cover his face like a cloud,
closing the day behind a mountain
                                        the eons have raised
between the generations.
The Journal. The Contact. The Courier.

The war we fight now is to understand.
On the other side of silent, untorn walls,
read the stories that you've told,
told back:

The Sheep Reports,
in which, one day, the razzia comes,
and men, like lambs, are rounded up,
herded to the town square, and marched
to the train that will take them to work,
in forced migration, from which some may return,
some not.
              She sees him, in among the others,
and runs into town, to his boss, to the mayor,
the kommandant, until her pure persistent energy
sparks the phone call that nets the slip of paper,
signed by the Fuhrer's bureaucrat,
freeing him.
                    Then runs returning to the station.
The men, now loaded, wait. The soldier
who halts her, smiles. She's pretty; it shows
in the photographs. They weren't all bad,
she'll say, and you'd do anything—but shudders
her distaste, stiffens after half a century
as his arm goes round her shoulder and he parades
the train's length with her, past faces frozen
in the windows, of men who are not
the fiancé whose name he's calling out—
the fiancé who doesn't respond
and rescue her, rescuing him.
Who isn't on the train....
                    He's slipped away,
is hiding in a neighbour stranger's cellar,
where many of his age return, still today.

Born to parents just freed from a war,
and raised through poor times, you stood ready
at the door to your own lives
when war blew open again.
                              And we were born to you,
in western calm, and overseas; have purchased
every available item, invented more
to serve invented needs, chased advertisements, flyers
memorized like biblical verse, with our arms
swung loosely round each other, talking, talking,
baffled by that part of you which always felt
so far away, subdued.

You bring him the paper, now, in his hospital room.
What happened fifty years ago still is news,
a living memory. It will live, later too,
but only as print.
                    I ask him, but no one cares
to hear about, he says, the Five-Day War,
that short workweek of fight when the Dutch withstood
invasion;
            about his company, trooping to a town
where snipers tried to pick them—their own: their own
were at the windows, behind the curtains, shooting.
It drove the Sergeant Major mad, who'd talked
of fording streams of blood, and dying for a cause.
He cracked: fired randomly, rapidly, in all directions,
wouldn't stop, until, my father says,
We had no choice: he had to be shot.

He had to be shot.
                    What happens happens
again, when events replay, and play the mind,
and the enemy is found alive

within that deadly loud report,
                                   and stinks fresh
memories of how he's redefined what's evil, sin;
and offers a hand to carry the sack
in which potatoes weigh each hard, right thing
you had no choice but do:
offers a chair, machine-rolled cigarette,
and with a warm, comradely grin
launches the innocent questioning.

And when the foreign occupiers, in full control,
moved their interrogations to another room,
they chose Burmania Huis, head office to a firm
that underwrote, in peace, policies for life
insurance.
                  The underground got it first,
the miserable joke, and snuck into the place ahead,
hid a microphone, and from their own small room
behind a bookstore selling Bibles, listened
as the questions climbed the stairs
to torture, and torture mounted
the tortured man; the weak
who surprised us, and didn't break,
or the strong who revealed a name.

There was a silence in each question, a silence
at the listening post behind the shelves
where guides to devotion, prayer books, stood;
a silence in the wheeling spokes of the bicycle,
quickly dispatched to the named one's home;
a silence that enwrapped the men
who worked beneath the war's surface,
bound in their committed silence,
a kind of marriage,

                              in which they rarely knew
each other's Christian name,
so that if their turn came to answer
they couldn't even taste the sweeter pleasure
of lying to the enemy's face,
but only truthfully deny it, say,
"I don't know him, friend."

And even after the war, he says, we rarely knew
or found who our friends had been,
who may have saved our lives.

And it hasn't all been filled, this silence.
And the cock still crows, three times at least
for every rising day,
                              and some, whom others
never blamed, weep
with the ones who rode the bike,
or who were named, and hid; with the ones
who didn't speak, but listened, closely,
to every word they would not choose to hear.

I know. It's some poor celebration, after fifty years,
to float the things that you preferred to slip
over the rail.
                              You married four months to the day
after Liberation, and later shipped with thousands
to the land those freeing soldiers came from.
It's from this country, too, our childhood stories
mostly come; as if some door had opened
and your lives could begin, but only after
the other door had shut, and an ocean filled
the dark room between.

An ocean
that for some of us, born here,
at times feels more like home
than here does.

But those sheep!
floating past the house, on New Year's Eve;
parading their dumb vulnerability
for all the twisted, darkened world
to see ...
I still think of them, their light
reflecting what little light there was, or is,
more and more.

Disarmament

After the cigar factory, the valley of sugar fields
and the nineteenth-century Spanish mansion
built on slave labour, our guide led us
into the Iglesia Parroquial de la Santísima Trinidad.
I half-expect to hear a four-piece Cuban band strike up
as I tell how my daughter removes her peaked cap,
out of respect, she'll explain to a friend back home,
and we listen to the story of a wooden altar,
one of many into which are carved
precise moments in the life of the Virgin Mary.
A young woman saunters by our group.
She looks surprisingly like a prostitute,
and a moment later Katie confesses
that she's given the woman her hat.
She pointed. She wanted it. What could I do?

My daughter seems pleased to have given away
something of her own, in this country of few possessions
and little money, but the white baseball cap
is her souvenir gift of last year's vacation,
when we carried our most recent possession—
her unexpected news—with us
like a piece of baggage we must fit
into the compact model of our family,
and I am not so generous.

She gives me her permission to tell this,
If I can read it first, she says, and to add
that in the old, barely kept-up Cuban church
another carved Mary entertains a holy dove
which hovers over her head, reminding Katie
of the Advent Sunday morning we heard
about the young woman's pregnancy, its origins
in the divine, when she leaned over my shoulder
and whispered, *That's what happened to me.*

What a scandal, Katherine, to profane
the gospel story with a joke.
But I laughed, because it *was* funny,
and you seemed so at peace, finally,
with yourself and with your pregnancy,
I began to wonder if the truth was not
the telling of that unlikely story
within a building the story helped to build,
that gave you permission. If, in that precise
moment, your baby became your honour,
what would I contradict?

Exiting the iglesia of the parish of Trinidad, Cuba,
we pass a small box balanced on a single wooden leg
like a crutch, and an elderly man making
eye contact, who points to a slot in the box top
as he repeats the phrase,
For the restoration ... For the restoration ...
I check for singles in my wallet
as our guide explains fathers are forbidden
to wear their white collars on weekdays,
in this country of equals—
but all I can find is a twenty.

The maracas, ancient muted trumpet, drums
and two guitars of a five-piece band
play for us at dinner, then move to entertain
later diners under the open plaza, who dance.
Mary and I are lying on the resort beach,
allowing the stars to reconcile the disparities
as we list the known facts:

our teenage daughter offering the white-
winged, souvenir baseball cap
to a streetwalker who asks for it,
inside a church where the walls weep
stains of infiltrating rainwater, within sight
of an altar honouring the impossible event
we are not hesitant to believe true
for her too,
so low had been her estate.

It is the old man's role to keep up the place
where this happens, where the paths of the two
sister-leads of the gospel drama
cross, asking after restoration.

I wish I'd given him the twenty.

Lying in your mother's bed, five hundred miles
from home, having come to see her
through her latest hospital stay,
you're feeling a little like a young blind puppy.
The ticking from her bedside timepiece
is louder, more richly mechanical than your own;
the rhythmic persistent push-pull, push-pull
of its internal clockwork,
that you imagine placing under the pillow.

Meanwhile, on the third-floor ward, your mother
in her almost inaudible hospital voice,
says, "I want to go home."
Her finger, though, is pointing toward the ceiling;
an action that so quickly depletes her body's strength
the arm soon falls
to lie beside her where she lies beyond the comfort
of her eternal working heart's
persistent push and pull.

I'm lying with you in your mother's bed,
a disconnected appendage, and I want to go home too.
I'm restless and dreaming we're on the third-floor deck
of the ferry crossing the Bay of Fundy.
Our centre of gravity here is somewhere below
and behind us, and we pivot, smooth and hugely,
on swells and plungers that pitch and tilt us
to radical angles, in a rhythm entirely arrhythmic,
unpredictable, that you'd never sleep a child to—
though it isn't unpleasant.

An obvious dream, I think, while dreaming it.
A great white wave tries to wake us, exploding
over the deck, and as the water pours down

the lounge windows, a woman your mother's vintage
labouriously stands, turns to her companion, and says,
"Unbelievable." And it is, in a manner of speaking.
She turns again, this time stepping toward the door,
and says she wants to see for herself
this ocean she and we and the Fundy ferry
are pushing through.

And turning in my dream of sleep as she turns to go,
I inadvertently assume the same position in which I saw
my father lie, half-curled against the bed-edge,
as if to enclose within himself the black the doctor said
he was so full of, blooming like phosphorescence.
Yet it seemed a kind of return, his sleeping shape.
It seemed so clear he was returning,
and that the place was hospitable he was returning to,
and this knowledge was contained within the pain-shaped form,
his unbetraying body.

I almost envied him his almost touching it,
the still and endless moment
when the moving vessel pulls to berth.

Goodnight Dad. Goodnight Mom. Goodnight
sweet sainted parents; mothers, fathers, all.
What more can you do than draw our fear away?
Goodnight.
And goodnight to all your parents' parents too.
You're not so complicated any longer, or taxed
by illness, age, infirmity, or us.
Goodnight.
Goodnight.

See you in the morning.

■ GIANTS

There used to be giants,
and they loved it here. They'd sit
their giant hinds in a row along the top edge
of the escarpment, and pick at the loose rock
with their hands or their feet, then throw or skip
the smoothest stones across the bay, to see who could land one
on the sandstrip, three miles away;

or they'd spring themselves off the scarp top
like you would off a low wall, and go running
all the way to the end of the sandbar,
and jump across the water to the other side,
or jump in, splashing and yelling up the ravines,
chasing each other's echoes.

This was only a few thousand years ago,
and the giants were still excited about the glaciers,
which were just leaving; about not having to wear
their coats all the time, and what
the ice and water had done, shaping and carving
this gentle, wild landscape!

They loved it here.

I'm telling you, they absolutely loved
every living minute here,

and they regretted ever having to leave.

Odds are, you'd say, by now Brock Road
should have worn itself into our mindscape;
like those paths, here, that before we came
everyone walked: the centuries' generous pounding
that sank them one foot, two feet down;
and the hills really happened, so did
the rock: go around.

                A year of travelling
its twelve short klicks, twice weekly, you'd say,
should have printed those barns, those houses,
the quarry and the crossroads, in sequence
on the brain. I wish. I want
history, and to ride it in my sleep.

Returning home, she tells me how it went, her summer
hour with the horses: tacking up, the outdoor ring;
oxer, bounce, cavalletti—and lately, wherever
she goes, can't help but break into canter, trot,
and jumps the white rail fence, plotting
a trail to ownership: these skills,
and something living, that much larger
than herself.
              At twelve years old, she feels the story
resolving to a landscape
she can love,
              that loves her desire,
but can't yet trust the hills desire
happens against, rock she must
move through,
                and by the 7th Concession Road
we've covered such familiar ground, at speed
you could wish some wishes met
                      that youngest inner drive

or need. The conversation slows, and like someone
whose own bruised geography
has never forgiven what
they did, I raise my foot
to every floating dreamscape underneath
and gently depress, braking

                              for the four-way stop.

   Above our heads
                    white buffalo, in casual
   slow stampede, move across the high blue plain.
   A flat-bellied herd we chase or follow
   to the jumping-off

                    of one day's history.

I love this road—twice weekly: its flat beeline
that rides the unremarkable hills that
only once in twelve short klicks
reach up to grab you in
the reproductive zone,

                    the intimate familiarity
that holds you to

                    the ground you spring from,
as in that split-second, near liftoff
you pray the earth

                    not, for pleasure,
end, ever.

He came to a place, the edge of a low bluff
overlooking the wide river of a dozen western movies,
and knew immediately that he'd always wanted
to cross one of these broad prairie rivers,
with its stone and pebble shallows,
the unknown strength and depth of its middle current,

on horseback (and he was on horseback),
and he knew, just as instantly,
that he couldn't take his stuff along—
the boxes covered in white canvas tied down with rope,
that had materialized out of the corner of his eye.
If he wanted to cross he'd have to leave it all behind.

He imagined his animal entering the shallows:
hooves on stones in running water;
the possible shifting underfoot,
the steady work against a heavy, downstream pull,
and rising, perhaps, on the other side. Dripping.
Would he look back? Probably.

There was no hint of irony,
no sense of this scene having played innumerable times before,
on innumerable screens, in every darkness.
He felt as though he was being provided
with a piece of information, visually:
a *You-are-here.*

That this circumstance required a decision from him
was where the moment lay.

He was happy with his dream,
and felt honoured by it.

What troubles him now, if trouble
is the word, is how the dream repeats.

In the church where we go to now a remnant people
fan themselves with the white paper wing of the bulletin,
on which is listed their comings and goings,
events, the summer schedule.

In the church where we go to now the white wings of seagulls
float among the rafters, above the sand,
where medieval castles of childlike construction,
that weren't there yesterday
and will be gone tomorrow,
are built and rebuilt,
subject to the rhythm and eternal Love of water.
People in low chairs line the shore,
observe the unmoving line of the horizon,
the motion of waves, the slow motions of the sky,
looking for signs, signs, signs—
though really they are not looking for anything at all.
Their present situation is quite sufficient.
The rhythm and eternal Love of water drew them here,
where the land ends and their faith stretches beyond limit,
and is quite sufficient.

In the church where we go to now a man and a woman
stand knee-deep in the water, talking,
allowing the lake to take its sweet, satisfying time.
They are talking Deep Ecology, Current Fiction, or fictions.
They are talking the Desert Fathers.
A beach ball makes a dash for freedom,
launching itself across the waves with the wind,
chased by a paddler on an air mattress,
past the third sandbar.
The paddler returns, rejoicing.
In any sanctuary, indoors or out,
the inscrutable parable of our childlike lives

is open to ongoing interpretation.
A man throws a tennis ball.
His young, long-haired Labrador bounds into the waves
and swims to shore holding in his jaws the fuzzy yellow pearl
it is clear he would gladly sell everything he owns
to retrieve.

Among the animals, it is our hairlessness
that stands out. In the holy, catholic church
there is no fear or shame. The godly walk and bask
beside the rhythm and eternal Love of water.
Bellies hang bulbous over the waistbands
of men whose jewels dangle in small pouches hung below,
like stones in a slingshot.
The round tops of numberless breasts abound,
leap from their halters. All that is hidden
will one day be revealed, and the day
seems very near.

The knee-deep man and the woman are still talking.
They are discussing if and how the surface tension of lake water
might bear their everyday weight.
The wind begins to rise.
Medieval castles of air and water
begin construction on the line of the horizon,
and as the people prepare to flee the wrath foretold,
they ask, *Will the weather always be so variable*
in the church where we go to now?
The white wings of seagulls hang in the rafters
as the seagulls wait for signs.
They land, filling the spaces left vacant by the departed.
They scream their screams for the departed,
picking at the sand for any trace,
their last communion with the departed.

I remember now. A family of four or six drives down the highway
on the last day of summer vacation, arguing and debating
where to stop to eat, where every day and meal
is a communion, one with the other,
and with the creatures of flesh who congregate the shoreline,
and with our eternal brother, who walked and basked upon
the rhythm and eternal Love of water,
that bids us, so appealingly, *Come.*

◾ HUMUS

The church where we go to now
is no big deal, a small group of protesters,
half a millennium after the fact,
in a city of need
in a hurried, wasteful time:
and it seems a kind of perverse luxury
that we experience so many varieties
of grief and sorrow
made available in such abundance,
though it doesn't quite fit
with the cut of our clothing,
or the cleanliness of our skin,
with only each other to fall back on,
after all, and our only righteousness
the love we bring,
and it is not for our perfections
that we are loved,
or the perfection of our gifts,
but only that we are, all, made
for this conversation, going on,
and now, having travelled
a dark passage
into this early morning light,
our eyes adjust,
we taste a kindness in the air,
this spring we smell
difference,
we catch an ancient scent, and
holy scat—
holy dog dirt on the lawn
after the snows are gone:
we've been pulled through.

We're only humus, after all.
And all the good we thought we were,
and all we did or did not do,
these seasons past,
is gone to soil, is
Holy. Holy. Holy.

If you sit on the third-floor balcony
of your twenty-six storey apartment building downtown,
you may find yourself staring down the barrel
of a twenty-five pounder gun, a howitzer,
positioned on the front lawn of the military museum
    across the street,
and feel perfectly confident that it is disarmed,
or hope so.

We carry no weapons here.
There is a formal requirement to love
    the one who stands beside the howitzer,
whether the howitzer be disarmed or armed,
and this keeps us in constant communication
with the unseen one who stands behind the one
who tomorrow may stand poised beside the howitzer.
For there is always the part in us
that considers the defence of our own bodies
    to be in our own hands,
that would avenge injustice,
the suffering of ourselves and others,
regardless of formal requirements.

And if they come with knife or fire,
or if the gun is held to my daughter's head,
if I and mine are driven into hiding under the High Level Bridge,
fleeing roundup, awaiting the inevitable
with others of our social, religious, ethnic
    or national community,
No, I do not beforehand know what my response will be.

Our lives run through our fingers like water.
Salt or red, the liquid drops that fall from our bodies,
the bodies of others,
fall onto the heated surface of current events.

The drops suffer and dance across the surface
and are released into the air.
They rise as the unseen vapour of supplication and intercession.
Our lives are the prayer given up against a cycle of violence.
The prayer forms a cumulo-witness,
condensing under the floor of heaven.

And you who read sky and radar screen,
who understand the behaviour of wind and cloud,
the markings on overhead jets—
how is it that you cannot detect the flight of the spirit,
my brother, my twin,
or where a reconciling rain might fall?

The war is never elsewhere.
The seeds of conflict float down on parachutes,
its roots run deep as dandelions
    in the front lawn of the military museum.
Our enemy currently lives behind a door
on the seventh floor of the same downtown apartment building.
He and his friends, male and female, toss bottles,
shout up and down from balcony to ground, at all hours,
keeping us in constant communication
with the unseen one who sits beside us on our balcony,
who lies beside us in our bed, listening.
Inevitably, the volume is turned up
as they dance to further taunt his formal requirement.

Tonight we lie awake,
and invite the spirit come brood over our twenty-six storeys,
the storied conflicts of a tired world.
To tuck us under wing, all.

Come, love,
disarm us.

Barbara, when Bart came by with the news,
we were taking down the garage.
You know the one, behind John and Martha's:
it's looked like a pushover for ages. Surprise.
That lilting twist along its spine, and the cockeyed
doorway that scared their car onto the drive
was only half the story. The other half
is how attached it was to living at that angle,
with no desire to fall, and no intent.

We went at the job with a sledgehammer,
and three different kinds of saw, their blades
dulling almost instantly against the building's
wonderful resistance. Then there stood Bart,
beside the dumpster we'd hired, with his son,
Wesley, who is eight. Why aren't all things and creatures
granted leave to take their own sweet time,
since it's so plain love alone maintains them?

Down the street, you were packing the last boxes
of your young family's move to Montreal,
when you first learned the news.
You must have entered your new home there,
and the physical reality of Donald's death, who'd gone
ahead of you, at just about the time we manhandled
the last jagged pieces of the garage's unwilling puzzle
into the bin, and swept up.

A friend and neighbour's yard is one big open
space now. We plan to fill it, soon,
with studs and rafters, true to the other's memory.
That's the easy part. Harder is
the work of love in monstrous vacancies
the heart had never planned to open to.
We wish that we could build you something there,
to house the jagged pieces, the emptied air.

In the church where we go to now
the time has come for redefinition.
For instance: *life everlasting*.
I'd like to think eternal being involves
the rock face exposed
by the highway blasted through,
and the possibility of slipping one's new, improved
body and soul
between the seams that divide time
from time,
to land on a beach
on the evening and the morning of the third day.

Ah! Creation.
It would be good. Very good.

I'd like to think that forever and ever and ever and ever
includes entering the cycle
whereby water congregates on the horizon as medieval castle
and is deconstructed, directly overhead,
into a million and one almost identically-sized parts
that simultaneously, one after the other,
fall.
I would ride the single drop on the windshield, in the
downspout,
jump the last few inches
and slip between the particles of earth,
descending to the root of darkness,
where I might rejoin my liquid kin,
and feel our urge to well
spring into pond, creek,
and be the river
running
to embody the lake;
and await the surface touch of fire

from ninety-three million miles,
and enter our star's fire,
the burn that prompts rising
re-congregation into the middle air ...

and begin again.

The one I love loves how it all goes round and round and round
the one I love is of the air, is of fire, of water, rock
dancing.

And if I am to be saved,
if my religion allows,
let it also be from this,
let me be saved from the ceaseless, unending,
eternal ways that I
and my body
constrict
in the face of this life,
which is love everlasting,
from how I and my body
gravitate, fall,
for that other lover, death.

The one I love
lives
in the air on fire under water through rock breathing liquid
molten flowing granite flames forever and ever and ever and ever
lasting.

Ah! Creation.

The one I love
The one I
The one

Notes

FORTY DAYS AND FORTY NIGHTS   Friesland, Groningen and Zeeland are provinces of the Netherlands; *luyden uit*, people from; *I rest me in the thought* ... is from the hymn "This is My Father's World" by F.L. Sheppard; *dorp*, village; *lucht in de band*, air in the tire, though *lucht* doubles as the word for both air and sky; *Canadees*, Canadian.

PEDLARS OF THE PRACTICAL   The Afsluitdijk (enclosing dike), completed in the 1930s, shut the Zuider Zee from the North Sea, and turned it into an inland lake, the Ijsselmeer. A portion of the former Zuider Zee, known as the Weiringermeer, had previously been enclosed by a dike and drained; *fietspad*, bicycle path; *netjes gedaan*, neatly done; *torens*, church towers; *taal*, language, tongue; *mijn man*, my man, i.e., husband; *Iedere Zondag*, every Sunday; *man en vrouw*, man and wife; *s'middags, na kerk*, afternoons, after church; *wandelde langs*, walked along, beside; *van de*, from the; *tot waar het andere*, to where the other; *toen het nog bos was*, when it was still woods, bush; *maar net alsof ze in de Prinsentuin liepen*, but just as though they were walking in the Prince's Garden. The park lies in the middle of Leeuwarden, the capital of Friesland.

RECORDINGS   *hemel*, heaven. The older churches in the Netherlands are often at the centre of town, and often encircled by a road. When organ recitals are recorded in them, the occasional sound of traffic may be heard on the finished product.

PATIENT OF DISCRETION   *kleine luyden*, literally, small people, or common folk; *vent*, fellow, guy; *Toch welbehagelijk* ... yet acceptable in your sight (see Psalm 19:14); *in koor gezongen*, sung in chorus; *weduwe*, widow; *timmerman*, carpenter; *onderwijzeres*, female teacher; *sangvogel*, songbird; *dominee*, pastor.

A PRAYER TO BE IN PARADISE WITH THE CHILDREN   after Frances Jammes' poem, "A Prayer To Be In Paradise With the

Donkeys," by way of Richard Wilbur's translation from the original French.

CAPTAIN KINTAIL   *Menno Simons (1496–1561)* begat the Mennonites, Protestant Christians, many of whom still "lead lives of great simplicity, both secularly and religiously," and often live in separate communities. *Milton Bradley* makes and sells *Balderdash*, a word definition game; *geep* is the invented word for a goat/sheep hybrid animal. *George McKibbon*, a land-use planner, maps areas that are significant or sacred to the various Ojibway and Cree bands in Northern Ontario. He uses these maps while advocating on behalf of the bands at hearings with the Ministry of Natural Resources and the commercial interests that wish to log, mine or develop hydroelectricity there. Edward "Buzz" Aldrin made public some twenty years later the contents of the personal pack (which each astronaut was allowed) that he carried on board the Apollo 11 flight to the moon.

Acknowledgements

My experience with the publishers of earlier books has been uniformly positive, and I would like to thank them by name: Pat de Jong, Peter Enneson, Mark Okkema and Don Sedgwick, for *Scrabbling for Repose*, with drawings by Richard Halstead (Toronto: Split Reed Press, 1982); Hennie Ruger and Joan Magee, for *Forty Days and Forty Nights*, *Naked Trees* and *Captain Kintail* (Windsor, ON: Netherlandic Press, 1987, 1990 & 1992); Marja Jacobs and Heather Cadsby, for *The Church Not Made With Hands* (Toronto: Wolsak & Wynn, 1997); David Kent, for *Devil's Punch Bowl* (Toronto: The St. Thomas Poetry Series, 1998); and Andrew Steeves and Gary Dunfield, for *Disarmament* (Kentville, NS: Gaspereau Press, 2003).

I would also like to thank some of the people who have been a source of encouragement and support along the way: William F. Blissett, Daphne Marlatt, Stan Dragland, Don McKay and Dennis Lee.

The same encouragement and support has come in my immediate community from Bryan Prince Bookseller, from Bryan himself, and Nancy, Tracy, Kerry and Andrew; the Hamilton Spectator; and the Hamilton Public Library, especially Beth Robinson.

Bringing things even closer to home, I want to thank the folks at St. Cuthbert's, especially Bart Nameth, who started many things, Cathy and Travis Stewart-Kroeker, Bob and Barb Hudspith, and Bill and Marta Vander Marel. And in the wider circle, Deborah Bowen and Daniel Coleman; Colin Macdonald and Glenn Macdonald; and Bernadette Rule, Marilyn Pilling, Linda Frank and Jeffery Donaldson.

Peter and Laura Enneson have been friends and cohorts for a long time. Nicholas, my brother, has borne much, with good cheer. Katie and Anna, my two daughters, continue to be an inspiration. And one more: Mary, heart of gold, thank-you.

Gaspereau Press acknowledges the support of the Canada Council for the Arts, the Nova Scotia Department of Tourism, Culture & Heritage and the Government of Canada through the Book Publishing Industry Development Program.

Typeset in Fred Smeijers' Quadraat and Quadraat Sans by Andrew Steeves and printed offset and bound under the direction of Gary Dunfield at Gaspereau Press, Kentville, Nova Scotia.

9 8 7 6 5 4 3 2 1

Library and Archives Canada Cataloguing in Publication

Terpstra, John
Two or three guitars: selected poems / John Terpstra.
ISBN 1-55447-027-7 (bound)
ISBN 1-55447-026-9 (pbk.)
I. Title.
PS8589.E75T86 2006   C811'.54   C2006-902852-4

GASPEREAU PRESS LIMITED
Gary Dunfield & Andrew Steeves □ Printers & Publishers
47 Church Avenue, Kentville, NS, Canada B4N 2M7
www.gaspereau.com